NBA Trivia Book

The Ultimate Basketball Trivia Questions for the Super-Fan

Copyright © 2021

All rights reserved.

DEDICATION

1. Which NBA team played at Amway Arena 1989-2010?

Answer: Orlando Magic

The Magic began at what was then called the Orlando Arena (1989-1999). That became the TD Waterhouse Centre (1999-2006) and The Arena In Orlando (2006) before being called the Amway Arena (2007-2010). The team then moved to the Amway Center in 2010.

2. Atlanta is the fourth home of the NBA's Hawks. Which of the following is NOT one of their previous locations?

- E. Moline, Illinois

- Milwaukee, Wisconsin

- St. Louis, Missouri

- Chicago, Illinois

Answer: Chicago, Illinois

The Hawks began their existence in 1946 as the Tri-Cities Blackhawks, playing their home games in East Moline's Wharton Fieldhouse. By 1951, the name had shortened to Hawks, and the franchise moved to Milwaukee, WI. In 1955 they called St. Louis, MO their home, and made the move to Atlanta in 1968. Among their famous stars of yesteryear were Don Otten, Bob Pettit, and Lenny Wilkens.

3. The Atlanta Hawks franchise joined the NBA in 1950. What was their franchise name in 1950?

Answer: Tri-Cities Blackhawks

Their first season in 1950-51 saw them as the Blackhawks. The following season, the team moved and became the Milwaukee Hawks until 1956. They then were the St. Louis Hawks where they won the franchise's first NBA Finals in the 1957-58 season. The franchise moved to Atlanta in 1969.

4. When I retired, I had played in more games than any other player, and won three rings as part of the Boston "Big Three" in the '80s. I have scored over 20,000 career points. Who am I?

Answer: Robert Parish

Robert Parish was the iron man of basketball. He played in 1611 games over 21 seasons in the NBA, winning three championships with the Boston Celtics. Parish finished his career with 23,334 points and over 14,000 boards.

5. Everyone knows about Dr. J, but do you know his real name?

Answer: Julius Erving

Julius Erving spent a couple of years in the ABA, but his entire NBA career was spent with the Philadelphia 76ers.

6. This player quite bluntly, put up some solid numbers in his career. He scored 38,387 points, grabbed 17,440 boards, and blocked 3,189 shots.

- Wilt Chamberlain

- Bill Russell

- Sheldon Lewis

- Kareem Abdul Jabbar

Answer: Kareem Abdul Jabbar

Kareem (who changed his name from Lew Alcindor) set a record for most points in a career, scored in 787 consecutive games, won MVP six times, was selected on The Defensive First Team five times, and acquired several other honors.

7. Who was the player who led the BAA in scoring in the league's very first season?

Answer: Joe Fulks

The BAA or "Basketball Assocation of America" is now known to many as the NBA (National Basketball Assocation). Fulks played for the Philadelphia Warriors avearging 23.2 ppg in the BBA's very first season(1946-1947). The Warriors won the BAA championship over the Chicago Stags 4-1 in the best of seven series.

8. What was the first team to have both the Slam Dunk contest and Three-point shootout champions in the same year?

Answer: Miami

During the 1995 All-Star Weekend, Glen Rice (then in his dominant years with the Heat) won the shootout and Harold Miner (aka Baby Jordan) won his second dunk contest in three years.

9. Who was the first player to record back-to-back 50 point games in the 2000s?

Answer: Antawn Jamison

Jamison recorded back-to-back 50 point games in the 2000-2001 season, while playing for the Golden State Warriors. The second of his two 50 point games came against the Lakers, in which Kobe Bryant also scored 50 points.

10. This 6-10 center won the MVP in back-to-back years in the early 80s with different teams. He also started a trend of going pro straight out of High School. Who was it?

Answer: Moses Malone

Moses won the NBA MVP twice with Houston in 79' and 82', and once with Philadephia in 83', the same year they won the championship.

11. Who was the undersized center on the Washington Bullets team that won the 1978 NBA Championship?

Answer: Wes Unseld

It was 6'7", 245-pound Wes Unseld who banged his way to the top in 1978, when Washington beat the Seattle Supersonics in the NBA Finals. Elvin Hayes was the power forward on the same team. Jack Sikma played center for Seattle in the series, and Bellamy played for several teams, but was retired by 1978.

12. Which two teams selected players ahead of Michael Jordan?

Answer: Houston and Portland

The year was 1984. Houston selected Hakeem Olajuwon, who went on to become great, and Portland selected Sam Bowie, who was plagued by injuries and never became an effective player. Jordan was selected third by Chicago and the rest is history.

13. Who was the first ever NBA lottery pick?

Answer: Patrick Ewing

1985 was the first year for the lottery. Before that they did a coin toss to determine one and two.

14. Who did Isiah Thomas punch in the back of the head, breaking his own hand?

Answer: Bill Laimbeer

Isiah and Bill were teammates for the Pistons.

15. How many times was Julius Erving an all star MVP?

Answer: 2

Julius Erving played in 11 all-star games. He was voted MVP in 1977 and 1983.

16. How many rules did Dr. Naismith start the game of basketball with?

Answer: 13

Some rules that seemed weird have been carried over, include the 5 men per team at all times rule. Therefore, if out of a team's 12 players, 7 foul out, and another person gets 6 fouls, he would be required to stay in the game. If due to injuries, a team cannot present 5 players, they cannot play 4 on 5, but rather forfeit the game. Last note: his original rules did not allow dribbling.

17. What is Wilt Chamberlain's record for most points in a game?

Answer: 100

Wilt set the record for most points on March 2, 1962 in Hershey, Pensylvania, vs. the New York Knicks.

18. What team won the 1956-57 championship?

Answer: Boston Celtics

The Boston Celtics won by 4 games to 3.

19. What was the original name of the NBA?

Answer: BAA

It is a little known fact that the NBA was called the Basketball Association of America until the early 1950's.

20. Between 1989 and 1998, how many different players won the NBA's rebounding title?

Answer: Three

Hakeem Olajuwon (1989-90), David Robinson (1991), and Dennis Rodman(1992-1998) were the only winners during this time.

21. Which one of these is not a 1st overall draft pick?

- Chris Webber

- Allen Iverson

- Kenyon Martin

- Dikembe Mutombo

Answer: Dikembe Mutombo

Dikemebe Mutombo was drafted fourth pick overall in the 1991 draft by Denver Nuggets.

22. Who was the first NBA player to score 2,000 points in a season?

Answer: George Yardley

George Yardley of the Detroit Falcons with 2,001 points in the 1957-58 season.

23. Why was the 1998 NBA Christmas Day game cancelled (the first-ever Christmas Day game that was cancelled)?

Answer: Lock Out

The NBA experienced a lockout in 1998, the third in its history, over the salary cap and players' wages. From July 1, 1998 - January 20, 1999, the owners staged a lockout and ultimately the season was shortened to 50 games. Another lockout occurred in 2011; that year the first NBA game of the season was played on Christmas Day.

24. In 1999, the Denver Nuggets shifted from McNichols Sports Arena to which facility?

Answer: Pepsi Center

Before the Pepsi Center, the Nuggets played at McNichols from 1975-1999. They were at the Denver Arena Auditorium 1967-1975. The Tacoma Dome was home to the Seattle Super Sonics 1994-1995. The Brooklyn Nets moved into Barclays Center in 2012.

25 The team known as the Sacramento Kings previously resided in all of the following cities EXCEPT:

- Rochester, NY

- Cincinnati, OH

- Kansas City, MO

- Oakland, CA

Answer: Oakland, CA

This club began as the Rochester Royals in 1948, moving to Cincinnati in 1957, and to Kansas City, where they became the Kansas City-Omaha Kings (of the Road) in 1972. Playing most of their home games in Kansas City,MO, with a few in Omaha, they made the move to Sacramento in 1985.

26. Who was the first NBA player to win five season MVP awards?

Answer: Bill Russell

The MVP Award began in the 1955-56 season. By the time that Russell of the Celtics won his fifth MVP in 1965, basketball great Wilt Chamberlain had won it only once.

27. I was drafted 1st overall in 1985 out of Georgetown. I played for three NBA franchises in my career, but never won a championship. I was also a part of the Dream Team. Who am I?

Answer: Patrick Ewing

Patrick Ewing is considered one of the greatest players to never get a ring, and is part of the 50 Greatest Players All-Time list. He scored 24,815 career points and swatted a great 2894 shots in his illustrious career. This center was also a member of the 1992 U.S. Dream Team.

28. Isiah Thomas was a basketball great that played for the Detroit Pistons. What was his number?

Answer: 11

Isiah Thomas played for the Pistons his entire career. He led Detroit to NBA Championships in 1989 and 1990 and was the Finals MVP in 1990.

29. This player is widely considered the greatest defender of all-time, but his rebounding numbers was what catches an eye. He set a record for most rebounds in a half, averaged 22.5 boards in 936 games, and set a career playoff record for most rebounds.

- Wilt Chamberlain
- Charles Barkley

- George Mikan

- Bill Russell

Answer: Bill Russell

Also highlighting Russell's Celtic career were his 11 NBA Championships and five MVP Awards. He was also a 12-time NBA All-Star.

30. Who was the only player who scored in the very first basketball game ever played with Dr. James Nasmith original 13 rules in Springfield, Massachusetts.

- Raymond P. Kaighn

- Henri Gelan

- Frank Mahn

- William R. Chase

Answer: William R. Chase

Out of the original 18 players, Chase was the only player to score.

31. In 1998, the Phoenix Suns roster had the #2 picks from the 1994 and 1995 draft (Jason Kidd and Antonio McDyess, respectively). Meanwhile, another team had the #3 picks from those very same drafts. Which team was it?

Answer: Detroit

The Pistons had Grant Hill (3rd pick in 1994) and Jerry Stackhouse (3rd in 1995), who had just come over in a trade from Philadelphia.

32. Who scored the first points of the millennium?

Answer: John Amaechi

Playing on New Year's Day 2000, the first game of the new millennium, the Miami Heat hosted the Orlando Magic. Magic center John Amaechi recorded the first basket of the game and millennium, and his jersey and shoes were taken to the Hall of Fame after the game.

33. Although a "bad boy" by reputation, this undersized power foward was one of the greatest rebounders of all-

time. During his career he played for three different teams, not including the two Olympic teams he played for in 1992 and 1996. His awards include 11 time all-star, All-Star MVP in 91', and league MVP in 93'. Who was it?

Answer: Charles Barkley

Charles was one of the first four players to have 20,000 points, 10,000 rebounds, and 4,000 assists in his career the other players as of the 03-04 season are Kareem Abdul-Jabbar, Wilt Chamberlain, and Karl Malone.

34. Who was the first center to lead the NBA in assists for a season?

Answer: Wilt Chamberlain

While playing with the Philadelphia 76ers, the high-scoring Chamberlain recreated himself and became the greatest passing center ever. In fact, in 1967-68, he led the league in total assists, being the only 20th century center to do so. He finished third in 1966-67, when the Sixers won the NBA Championship.

35. Who was the first player to average a triple double thoughout an entire regular season?

Answer: Oscar Robertson

"The Big O" is considered one of the best all around players ever in the league. He and Kareem Abdul Jabar led the Bucks to and NBA championship in 1971.

36. Who was the first ever unrestricted free agent?

Answer: Tom Chambers

Tom went to Phoenix in 1988.

37. Who represented the 'M' in the trio known as "Run TMC"?

Answer: Mitch Richmond

The high octane trio affectionately known as "Run TMC" consisted of Tim Hardaway, Mitch Richmond, and Chris Mullin. They led the Golden State Warriors to several exciting playoff runs during the early 1990s.

38. For what team did Oscar Robertson play for the majority of his career?

Answer: Cincinnati Royals

Oscar Robertson played the majority of his career with the Cincinatti Royals, but closed his career with the Milwaukee Bucks.

39. What year was Wilt's 100 point game?

Answer: 1962

The famous game in Hershey, PA is surrounded by mystery and intrigue. One thing is for sure though, the NBA saw the greatest single performance in its history.

40. Who was the winner of the 1976-77 NBA MVP?

Answer: Kareem Abdul-Jabbar

Kareem held the record for most points over a career with 38,387.

41. When did Kobe Bryant set a record fo beating 12 Three-Pointers in a game?

Answer: January 7, 2003

Kobe Bryant did it against the Seattle Super Sonics where they won.

42. Who won the first championship when the league changed its name to the NBA?

Answer: Minneapolis Lakers

Although the Philadelphia Warriors won the first ever championship of the BAA, the Minneapolis Lakers won the first championship when the league changed into the NBA in the 1949-1950 season. The Lakers were led by the great George Mikan.

43. How many scoring titles did Wilt Chamberlain win during his career?

Answer: Seven

Wilt had an amazing career, including 15 of the top 20 individual scoring games.

44. What school was Tim James drafted from?

Answer: Miami

Tim James was drafted from UM by the Miami Heat 25th pick overall of the 1999 NBA Draft.

45. How many times did Wilt Chamberlain score fifty or more points in a NBA game?

Answer: 118

Wilt scored seventy or more points four times.

46. The first Christmas Day game in the NBA featured the Providence Steamrollers. Who was their opponent at the game held at Madison Square Garden?

Answer: New York Knicks

The Knicks won the game 89-75. Back then the teams chosen

to play were typically local rivals. This was done to shorten the travel time to and from the game in order to make sure the players could have more family time. Now the teams chosen to play the Christmas game typically have the best records. In many cases one of the games features the two teams from the previous year's playoffs.

47. For the 1971-72 season, the San Diego Rockets became the Houston Rockets and relocated to which place?

Answer: Hofheinz Pavillion

The Houston Rockets played at Hofheinz Pavillion through the 1974-75 season. They then moved to The Summit from 1975-2003 (The Summit was renamed the Compaq Center in

1998). In 2003, the Rockets relocated to the Toyota Center. The Wells Fargo Center became home to the Philadelphia 76ers in 1996.

48. The club currently known as the Houston Rockets originated in....

- Toledo, OH

- Huntsville, AL

- They have always been in Houston

- San Diego, CA

Answer: San Diego, CA

The expansion franchise placed in San Diego, CA was named the Rockets, and played there from 1967 through 1971, when they fittingly moved to Houston, TX. The other cities mentioned have college teams named Rockets.

49. The Boston Celtics won the NBA Championship for the 2007-08 season. Who did they defeat?

Answer: Lakers

The Celtics won their 17th NBA Championship four games to two. Paul Pierce was the MVP of the finals.

50. Some consider me the best defender of all-time and one of the top centers of my time. I spent my entire career with one team, winning 11 championships. Who am I?

Answer: Bill Russell

Bill is probably the greatest big man of all-time. Not only did he rank second in all-time rebounds with 21,620, but he also has a record 11 championships, and has won 5 MVP awards. He spent all of his career with the Celtics too.

51. With what team did Wilt Chamberlain spend the lastpart of his NBA career?

Answer: Los Angeles Lakers

Wilt Chamberlain was best known for his career with the Lakers. He wore number 13.

52. Many call me, "the first great center". I was the first to perfect and utilize hook shots. I led my team to 5 NBA Championships as well. I wore #99. Who am I?

Answer: George Mikan

Mikan was one of the first real dominant players of the game, he led the Minneapolis Lakers as their lead scorer, rebounder, and their tallest player.

53. What was the original name of the ABA (American Basketball Assocation) Denver Nuggets?

Answer: Denver Rockets

The Rockets did not change their name to the Nuggets until the 1974-1975 season. The Nuggets were one of four ABA teams to go to the NBA when the league folded after the 1976 season. The Spurs, Nets, and the Pacers were the three other team from the ABA to go to the NBA.

54. The top three vote-getters for 1996-97 Rookie of the

Year all wore number 3. The following season, the first two All-Stars from that draft class both wore what other number?

Answer: 8

Allen Iverson won 1997 Rookie of the Year, with Stephon Marbury and Shareef Abdur-Rahim (all wearing number 3) coming second and third in votes. The following year, none of these three were in the All-Star game, and the only players drafted the previous year to make it on were Kobe Bryant and Antoine Walker (both number 8).

55. Who were the first two undrafted rookies in NBA history to make the All-Rookie 1st or 2nd team?

Answer: Udonis Haslem and Marquis Daniels

Haslem and Daniels were both named to the All-Rookie 2nd team in 2003-2004, the first rookies to do so. Haslem, a former University of Florida Center went undrafted in the 2002 draft, but was picked up by the Heat after spending a year overseas. Daniels was not picked in the 2003 draft, but was quickly signed by the Mavericks and went on to come up huge at the end of the regular season and playoffs for Dallas.

56. This player was one of the most feared men to shoot against in the 70s. He was 7-2 and a massive afro that made him look even taller. During his career he recorded over 1,700 blocks with the Bulls, Spurs, and the Celtics. Before coming to the NBA he played 4 seasons with the Kentucky Colonels of the ABA.

- Wilt Chamberlain

- Bill Russell

- Julius Erving

- Artis Gilmore

Answer: Artis Gilmore

At 7-2, 240lbs., some say Artis Gilmore was the strongest man to ever play the game, as he was a threat to block every shot.

57. Who was the starting center on the Chicago Bulls 1991-1992 roster?

Answer: Bill Cartwright

Remember the tall, tired-looking old man with the gray goatee? It was Bill Cartwright, number 24. He didn't score or rebound, nor did he block shots, but he was there alright.

58. How many NBA titles did Magic Johnson win in his career with the Lakers?

Answer: 5

Magic won in 1980, 1982, 1985, 1987 and 1988. He is definitely one of the best all time players with career averages of 19.5 points per game and 11.2 assists per game.

59. In which year did Lenny Wilkens win coach of the year honors?

Answer: 93-94

On January 6, 1995, Wilkens became #1 in coaching victories with 939.

60. Dennis Rodman concluded his career in 2000 with how many championship rings?

Answer: 5

Rodman earned his nickname "The Worm" for his defensive prowess, tenacious reboounding, and intense scrappiness as a member of 5 NBA championship winning teams: Detroit Pistons (1988-1989 & 1989-1990); Chicago Bulls (1995-1996, 1996-1997, & 1997-1998).

61. Which one of these players is one of the fifty greatest NBA players of all-time?

- Gail Goodrich

- Bob Lanier

- Walt Bellamy

- Clyde Drexler

Answer: Clyde Drexler

Although all of the players are in the hall of fame, only Clyde 'the Glide' Drexler was one of the fifty greatest players of all time. He wore the #22 most of his career.

62. Which of these name combinations do not represent the same person?

- Lew Alcindor - Kareem Abdul-Jabbar

- Brian Williams - Bison Dele

- Olivier St. Jean - Tariq Abdul-Wahad

- Chris Johnson - Mahmoud Abdul-Rauf

Answer: Chris Johnson - Mahmoud Abdul-Rauf

Mahmoud Abdul-Rauf is actually Chris JACKSON, who was an outstanding player at LSU before joing the pros. His most productive stints were at Denver and Sacremento, before ending his career at Vancouver with fellow Muslim Shareef Abdul-Rahim.

63. Who was the first player to win back to back MVPs?

Answer: Bill Russell

Bill Russell won a total of five MVPs over his career with the Boston Celtics.

64. Which player was 9 for 9 from three point range in a game in 2003?

Answer: Latrell Sprewell

Latrell Sprewell made it in Febuary 4, 2003.

65. Which of the following players averaged over 20 rebounds per game in their career?

- Dennis Rodman

- George Mikan

- Spud Webb

- Bill Russell

Answer: Bill Russell

Bill Russell averaged over 20 rebounds a game during the course of his career, winning 11 championships in the process with the Boston Celtics.

66. True or False: Shaquille O'Neal won an NBA scoring title on the Orlando Magic?

Answer: True

In 1995 Shaq averaged 29.3 points per game and won the scoring title.

67. Which one of these Laker numbers was retired last (afater the other three)?

- 33

- 32

- 13

- 34

Answer: 34

32 Magic Johnson, 33 Kareem Abdul-Jabbar, 13 Wilt Chamberlain.

34 is Shaq's uniform Number.

68. Who was the first lottery pick in NBA history?

Answer: Patrick Ewing

Patrick Ewing, New York Knicks, 1985

69. Who was the first NBA player to score 60 points in a Christmas Day game, doing so in a contest between the Knicks and the Nets?

Answer: Bernard King

In 1984 Bernard King played for the New York Knicks; the Christmas Day game that year featured the Knicks against the New Jersey Nets. It was a stellar season for the future Hall of Famer. He ended the season as the NBA Scoring Champion and on the All-NBA First Team for the second year in a row.

70. At the beginning of the twenty-first century, which of these arenas was the oldest still in use?

- The BMO Harris Bradley Center

- The Palace Of Auburn Hills

- The Target Center

- The Oracle Arena

Answer: The Oracle Arena

The Oracle Arena in Oakland, California became home to the Golden State Warriors in 1966. The Milwaukee Bucks began at the BMO Harris Bradley Center in 1988. Also in 1988, The Palace of Auburn Hills, in Auburn Hills, Michigan, began hosting the Detroit Pistons. The Minnesota Timberwolves moved into the Target Center in Minneapolis in 1990.

71. The team currently known as the Los Angeles

Clippers was originally known as the:

- San Diego Conquistadors

- Baltimore Bullets

- Oakland Clippers

- Buffalo Braves

Answer: Buffalo Braves

The Buffalo Braves were an expansion franchise that joined the NBA in 1970, along with the Cleveland Cavaliers, and the Portland Trail Blazers. The club left Buffalo in 1978 and moved to San Diego, CA where they were known as the San Diego Clippers (no relation to the Conquistadors of the old ABA).In 1984, they moved to Los Angeles and became the

L.A. Clippers.

72. Who was the first-ever number one overall draft pick in NBA history in 1950?

Answer: Chuck Share

Share was drafted by the Boston Celtics, but never played a game for them. He played for Fort Wayne in the 1951-52 season, then the Hawks in 1954. After the Hawks, Chuck was a one-season Minneapolis Laker and retired in 1960. He averaged 8.3 points and 8.4 rebounds in his career.

73. This great center dominated the post in the early days of pro basketball, and was the first big man to make a big prescence. Multiple scoring titles highlight this player's career. He passed away in 2005. Who is he?

Answer: George Mikan

George was the first big man to dominate. At 6ft 10in (2.08m) He was quite tall for for the era that he played in the 1940s and 1950s for Minneapolis Lakers . He wore the number 99.

74. Which of these players retired with the most points scored in their career?

- Oscar Robertson

- Clyde Drexler

- Bill Walton

- Kareem Abdul-Jabbar

Answer: Kareem Abdul-Jabbar

Kareem Abdul-Jabbar scored 38,387 points in his lifetime. He also had a record six MVPs.

75. This player grew up in Nigeria and was said to have never even picked up a basketball until age 17. On March 29, 1990, he had an amazing quadruple-double against the Milwaukee Bucs.

- Dikembe Motumbo

- Shareef Abdur-Rahim

- Patrick Ewing

- Hakeem Olajuwon

Answer: Hakeem Olajuwon

In Olajuwon's outstanding outing against the Buc's, he had 18 points, 16 rebounds, 10 assists, and 11 blocked shots. Also among his career honors were: Two NBA Titles, one MVP Award, a member of the All-NBA First Team six times, and the All-NBA Second Team three times.

76. In which city did basketball debut as an Olympic sport?

Answer: Berlin

The first year when basketball was an Olympic sport was in 1936. USA won the Gold the very first time basketball was an Olympic sport with Canada getting the silver.

77. In the 1984 draft, the third and fourth picks were used on a shooting guard and a power forward from

North Carolina (Michael Jordan and Sam Perkins, respectively). Strangely, this exact same statement could apply to the 1995 draft as well. Jerry Stackhouse was picked third by Philadelphia. What UNC teammate of his went immediately after to Washington?

Answer: Rasheed Wallace

Interesting note: a very similar scenario occurred in the 1998 draft as well, with North Carolina power forward Antawn Jamison going fourth, and shooting guard Vince Carter going fifth. Useless but interesting.

78. Who was the first coach in NBA history to lead a team to an under .500 record, and win Coach of the Year in the same season?

Answer: Johnny Kerr

Johnny Kerr coached the expansion Chicago Bulls to a 33-48 record in their inaugural season, earning him the Coach of the Year honors.

79. Which of these retired guards had the most career assists?

- Nate Archibald

- Lenny Wilkins

- Jerry West

- Maurice Cheeks

Answer: Maurice Cheeks

Maurice Cheeks, the coach of the Portland Trail Blazers in 2004, had 7,392 career assists. Lenny Wilkins had the second most of those listed with 7,211.

80. Who was the intense, nasty center on the Detroit Pistons Bad Boy team of the late eighties and early nineties, who wore number 40?

Answer: Bill Laimbeer

Laimbeer busted quite a few chops in his day. Even Robert Parish, the calm, quiet Celtics center had lowered himself to hitting Laimbeer in the face, after receiving several elbows from the infamous Motor City Bad Boy.

81. Which team did Lenny Wilkens lead to an NBA

Championship?

Answer: '79 Supersonics

Wilkens only won one championship and one coach of the year award.

82. In Game 5 of the 1994 Eastern Conference Finals, Reggie Miller single-handedly led the Indiana Pacers to a come from behind victory against the New York Knicks, at their fabled Madison Square Garden. How many points did he score in the 4th quarter alone?

Answer: 25

To add to the drama of this exciting series, Reggie Miller taunted the New York crowd, particularly life-long New

Yorker Spike Lee. In the game's closing moments Miller paced towards Lee, and expressed the now infamous "choke-hold". Ironically, the Pacers went on to lose Game 7, and the series at Madison Square Garden.

83. Which one of these players was not a first round NBA draft pick?

- Walt Frazier

- Bob Pettit

- Robert Parish

- George Gervin

Answer: George Gervin

In the ABA he was selected in the first round, but in the

NBA he was selected in the third round of the 1974 Draft by San Antonio Spurs.

84. Which of the following players is the son of Jimmy Walker?

- Samaki Walker

- Antoine Walker

- Tony Dumas

- Jalen Rose

Answer: Jalen Rose

An interesting story has always been Rose's relationship with his father. Never having known him too well, he has gone by his career rather than his personal life.

85. Which team was the first to win back to back NBA titles?

Answer: Minneapolis Lakers

The Lakers won their first two titles beating the Syracuse Nationals and the Washington Capitols. The Lakers won both series 4-2. They won in the 1948-49 and the 1949-50 seasons.

86. Who in 2003 became the youngest player to reach 10,000 points mark?

Answer: Kobe Bryant

Kobe Bryant made it in his 24th years old and 193 days.

87. Which team did Wilt Chamberlain play on before his time with the Philadelphia Warriors in the 1958-1959 season?

Answer: Harlem Globetrotters

Most people associate Wilt "the Stilt" with the Los Angeles Lakers. He played 5 seasons with the Lakers, four years with the Warriors of Philadelphia and San Francisco, and three with the 76ers. However, in the 1958-1959 season, Wilt was seen touring with the Harlem Globetrotters.

88. These two rookies were named MVP of the league in their rookie years. They were both drafted in the 1960s. Who are they?

Answer: Chamberlain, Unseld

Wilt the Stilt (1960) and Wes Unseld (1969) were both dominant centers. No other rookie had achieved this feat by the end of the 20th century.

89. Which of these played with Tim Duncan?

- Jerry Stackhouse

- Ken Johnson

- Jeff Foster

- Loren Woods

Answer: Loren Woods

Loren Woods played with Tim Duncan in Wake Forest in 1996.

90. Who had the highest points per game average for a rookie in NBA history?

Answer: Wilt Chamberlain

Wilt Chamberlain of the Philadelphia Warriors with 37.6 ppg in season 1959-60.

91. Which one of the following participated in the NBA Christmas Day game as both a player and a coach?

- Red Auerbach

- Bill Walton

- Pat Riley

- Phil Jackson

Answer: Phil Jackson

According to a 2010 article in "The New York Times", Jackson has been involved in at least 20 Christmas Day NBA games as a player (New York Knicks and New Jersey Nets) and as a head coach (Chicago Bulls and Los Angeles Lakers). In fact, he was a fixture as a coach on the Christmas Day game, participating in every game but two from 1990-2011. To date, he is the fastest NBA coach to win 1000 games, doing so at the game on Christmas Day in 2008. Doc Rivers also has participated in the game as a player (New York Knicks) and coach (Boston Celtics).

92. At which place did the Atlanta Hawks NOT have home court advantage? [There is a hint in the question.]

Answer: Kiel Arena

The Atlanta Hawks were at the Omni Coliseum 1972-1997, the Georgia Dome 1997-1999, and Philips Arena beginning in 1999. The St. Louis Hawks played at Kiel Arena from 1955-1968, then relocated to Atlanta. The Atlanta Hawks played at the Alexander Memorial Coliseum from 1968-1972.

93. The club currently known as the Washington Wizards has previously been known as all of the following EXCEPT:

- Chicago Packers

- Chicago Zephyrs

- Baltimore Bullets

- Washington Senators

Answer: Washington Senators

The NBA's first true "expansion" team was placed in Chicago in 1961 and dubbed the Packers (presumably as homage to the city's meatpacking history). Possibly because of Windy City sports fans dislike of a rival football team with the same name, they stayed away from the decrepit Chicago Coliseum in droves. A name change the next year to the Zephyrs didn't help, and the club picked up and moved to Baltimore after only 2 seasons in Chicago, where they resurrected the name Baltimore Bullets from a club that had played there in the early '50's. Washington Senators was the name of the baseball team that is now the Texas Rangers.

94. What was Kareem Abdul-Jabbar's born first name?

Answer: Ferdinand

Kareem was born Ferdinand Lewis Alcindor Jr. in 1947. After attending UCLA, he joined the Milwaukee Bucks in 1969 and played with them for six seasons. His other 14 seasons were with the Lakers. He won a season MVP six times, and retired in 1989 with the most points scored in NBA history with 38,387. On May 1, 1971, Alcindor changed his name to Kareem Abdul-Jabbar. Kareem was inducted into the Hall of Fame in 1995.

95. This combination of centers was known as the Twin Towers back in the day. Both men were at least seven feet playing on the same NBA team. One half of this

dynamic duo went on to rank 7th in all-time scoring. Who are they?

Answer: Hakeem Olajuwon / Ralph Sampson

This giant combination of Hakeem "The Dream" Olajuwon and Ralph Sampson made big impact during their time together on the Rockets. Hakeem went on to score 26,946 points and become one of the top centers ever.

96. What team was lucky enough to have defensive great Bill Russell for his entire career?

Answer: Boston Celtics

Bill Russell was one of the most amazing defensive centers in NBA history. Bill was an MVP five times in his career (1958,

1961, 1962, 1963 and 1965).

97. In my 17 year career I averaged 21.0 points, 9.8 rebounds, and 2.45 blocks over 1,138 career games. I also was a number one overall draft pick. Who am I?

Answer: Partrick Ewing

Some of Ewing's astounding career highlights include 51 points in a game, 26 total rebounds in a game, the New York Knicks all-time leading scorer at the time of his retirement, Rookie of the Year in 1986, and part of the All-NBA First Team in 1990.

98. Which school won the very first NCAA National Championship for Men's Basketball?

Answer: Oregon

Oregon won the NCAA Men's Basketball championship in 1939. The Ducks beat out Ohio State with the final score of 46-33.

99. During the 1994 All-Star Game, half of the Eastern Conference roster was made up of players from what two teams?

Answer: Chicago and New York

Each team had three players on the Eastern squad (to make up 6 of the 12 players representing the East): Chicago sent Scottie Pippen (who was MVP of the game), Horace Grant and B.J. Armstrong, while New York sent Patrick Ewing, Charles Oakley and John Starks. Add two New Jersey Nets to that (Derrick Coleman, Kenny Anderson), and that left only four spots for the other 11 teams to fill. It is usually unlikely a team will have two, let alone three all-stars on their roster in the same year, so this was a pretty memorable factoid.

100. Who was the first top five pick from Florida State in NBA Draft history?

Answer: Dave Cowens

Cowens was selected 4th overall in the 1970 draft, while Sura was the 17th overall pick in 1995, Charlie Ward was taken 26th overall, and while Joe Smith was taken #1 Overall, he attended the University of Maryland, not Florida State.